Rodney Legg is the chairman of the Open Spaces Society. Formerly and formally the Commons, Open Spaces and Footpath Preservation Society – founded in 1865 – it is Britain's oldest national conservation body.

Here Legg researches his predecessors' efforts that led to them founding the National Trust, as an offshoot to the Commons Preservation Society in 1895. In the first half of the twentieth century the society, through appeals and the gifts of its members, was directly instrumental in securing 5,000 acres of endangered commons, heath and other open land, which were then vested in the ownership of the National Trust

Legg is a member of the Trust's ruling council and its access review working party. Born in 1947 he is a professional historian, working mainly on archaeological, military and West Country subjects. He has also published many collections of circular walks and ends this little study firmly on the ground, with an appraisal of the Trust's next objectives and opportunities.

NATIONAL TRUST CENTENARY

Common roots of 1895

Rodney Legg

Wincanton Press
National School, North Street,
Wincanton, Somerset BA9 9AT

For Sir John Smith –
who brought me back
into the fold

First published 1994.
Copyright Rodney Legg © 1994
Permission is hereby given for extracts to be quoted by
anyone researching the history of the National Trust,
provided that the source is acknowledged.

Printed in Somerset
by FWB Printing at Wincanton
Distributed by the Wincanton Press
telephone 0963 32583, until 1995, then 01963 32583
International standard book number 0 948699 39 6

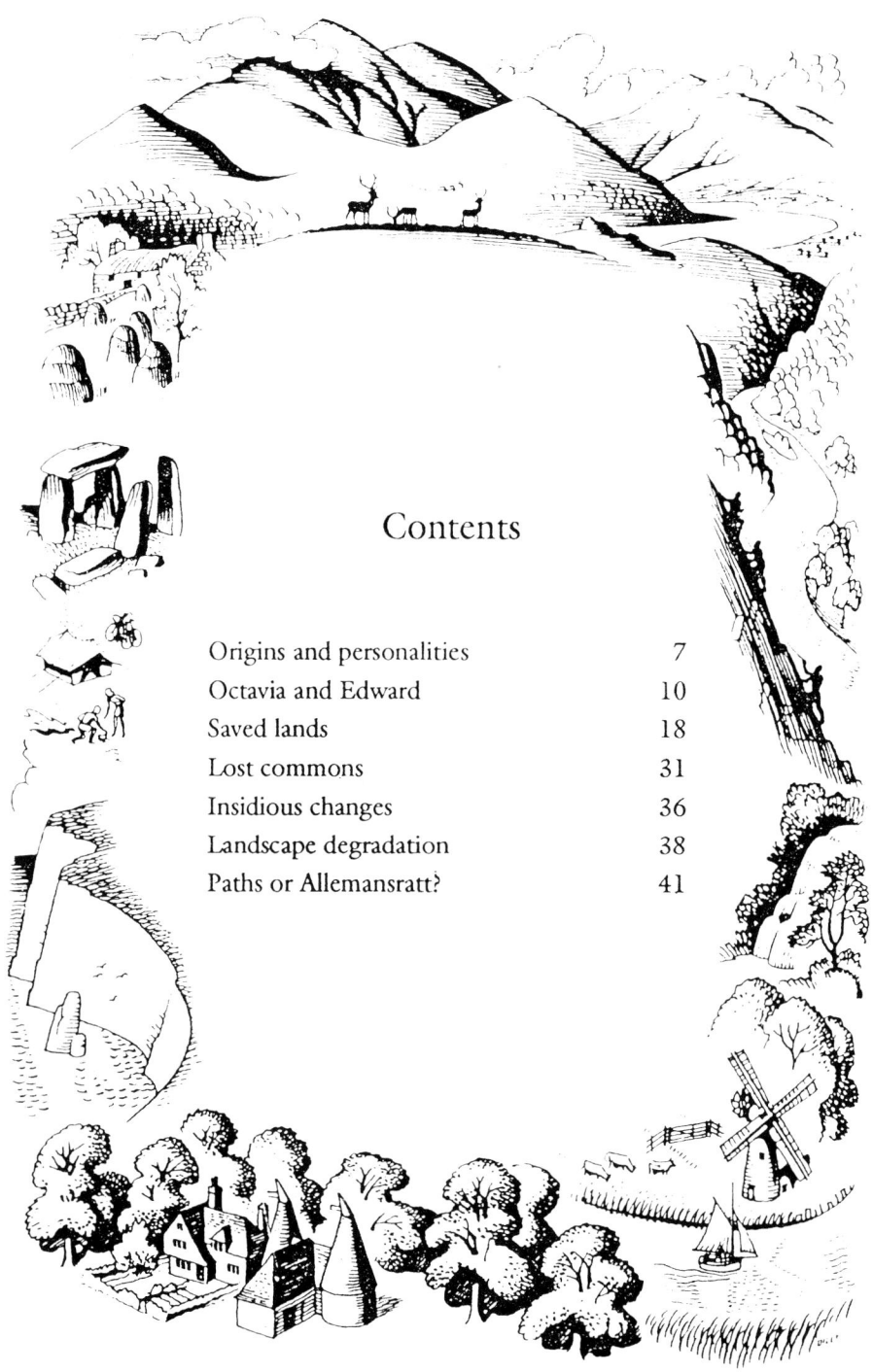

Contents

Origins and personalities	7
Octavia and Edward	10
Saved lands	18
Lost commons	31
Insidious changes	36
Landscape degradation	38
Paths or Allemansratt?	41

"HOW TO MAKE A SOCIALIST."

Knowing he is too poor to go to law—steal his bits of Common and shut him out.

Then stop his footpaths. [From "*Fun*," 28/12/87.

Origins and personalities

The National Trust has its beginnings in the wealthy Victorian backlash against developments that were robbing London of suburban open spaces. Those concerns were first articulated on behalf of residents and what became the open-air movement by a 34-year-old lawyer, George John Shaw-Lefevre, who called a meeting at his chambers in the Inner Temple and founded the Commons Preservation Society on 19 July 1865.

This has the distinction of being Britains's first national conservation body. Shaw-Lefevre immediately gathered a committee of considerable talent and distinction. His colleagues included the barrister Charles Edward Pollock, who would be instrumental in rescuing Wimbledon Common, and Sir Thomas Fowell Buxton, Liberal MP for King's Lynn, who would lead the campaign that saved Epping Forest.

Their intellectual mentors, appearing in person, were Professor Thomas Henry Huxley, science lecturer and the first eminent champion of Charles Darwin's hypothesis *On the Origin of Species*, and libertarian philosopher John Stuart Mill, at the peak of his fame with all his books written and now allowing himself to be elected to Parliament without having to trouble to do any soliciting for votes beyond a week of addressing meetings.

The rising generation was represented by Leslie Stephen, the editor of the Cornhill Magazine and future father in 1882 of Virginia Woolf, and "*the nice young lawyer*" Edward Bond MP who would in 1877 become briefly engaged to Octavia Hill, who was also deeply concerned in the work of the Commons Preservation Society which, she found, brought "*a pleasant sense of friction and stimulus, though none of peace*". Parallel to this, with the help of her sisters, in 1878 Miss Hill founded the Kyrle Society "*with the aim of placing objects of beauty within the reach of the poor*".

Those places of beauty included Burnham Beeches, the gardens of London squares, and disused burial grounds. Typical of the campaigns was that to save Bunhill Fields, where Bond,

Hill and Shaw-Lefevre took on the Society of Friends and tried to save from "*bricks and mortar*" or "*hideousness of neglect*" what was the last inner-city open space in the East End of London. The Quakers defied Octavia, the local vicar, and the people, by deciding to take the money and build. Or so it is recorded, but present-day Quakers feel that Octavia might have protesteth too much.

Following the example of the Romans, Parliament enacted in 1855 that future London cemeteries were to be established on green field sites beyond the urban building lines. Existing graveyards were to be closed. These included Bunhill Fields where an unused 1665 Plague-pit had been subsequently taken over by non-conformists. That burial ground contains a host of dissenting ministers and their congregations – notably John Bunyan, Daniel Defoe, Isaac Watts, and William Blake.

Adjoining is the Quaker burial ground which pre-dated the 1665 pandemic. Sold by Sir Reginald Foster, in October 1661, for £270, it was the first freehold land to be acquired by the Society of Friends. This original plot, off Chequer Alley, is said by Quaker historian George Edwards to have been about 90 square yards – a suitable site for just one house: *"The original plot of land was soon full. During the next 200 years Friends acquired adjoining tenements; these were either let to tenants or occupied by poor Friends, till demolished in order to make use of the ground on which they stood for burials."*

In Victorian times the law forced its closure, Edwards writes: *"Friends were left with a disused burial ground which had never had a meeting house attached, the problem was what to do with the land. A part was sold for erecting a school, while a strip was compulsory purchased to widen Coleman Street [now Roscoe Street], any human remians disturbed were reinterred in another part of the ground. As Friends had not allowed memorial stones to be placed on individual graves it is not possible to identify any particular grave, but tradition has always said that George Fox was buried about where the memorial stone has recently been placed."*

More than 12,000 were buried there and the land remained the principal place of Quaker pilgrimage. In 1874, a 19-year-old with missionary zeal, Joseph Bevan Braithwaite, erected a marquee that seated 300 people. He replaced it with "an Iron Room" and then the "Memorial Hall" which with classrooms, a coffee tavern and a tennis court became an extensive complex for religion, education, and leisure. Part was leased to the Bedford Institute which was to organise the first adult schools in London. Young Braithwaite's ambitious plans may well have sparked Octavia Hill into strident opposition.

Richard Harland, a Yorkshire Quaker who is an executive committee member of the Open Spaces Society, went to Bunhill Fields in 1993 to see if there was any obvious explanation for Octavia Hill's concern: *"I am puzzled as I found what I believe to be the Quaker burial ground serving as a fine open space whereas the non-conformist one next door was locked and barred (though possibly for the night only)."*

The Bedford Institute was destroyed by German bombs in the Second World War. A surviving caretaker's house became the Friends' Meeting House and the remainder of the land was leased to Finsbury Council for a garden of rest and replacement tennis court.

George Edwards records that the Quakers still own the land: *"The Six Weeks Meeting, which is the Finance and Property Committee of London and Middlesex Quarterly Meeting, who have always been the owners of the burial ground, still retain the freehold."*

1—The Common Stile.
There should be two risers: one 15 inches from the ground, and the other 12 inches higher. This stile affords seats.

Octavia and Edward

It was in 1877 that 38-year-old Octavia Hill and 33-year-old Edward Bond came as close as either would come to marriage. Bond, it seems, had everything to offer. His charm, fine physique and great riches made him, according to Beatrice Webb, *"the beloved of the philanthropic set"*. He was fascinated by Octavia's big brown eyes that *"missed nothing and would flash devastating disapproval"*.

Octavia and Edward were joint secretaries of a committee that raised £9,000 *"to purchase the fields lying between the Swiss Cottage and Hampstead, with the view of preserving them for public use"*. On 29 October 1875 they had written to the secretary of the Commons Preservation Society, Edward Fithian, suggesting that *"it would not be inappropriate if your society were to enlarge the scope of its action and add to its objects the acquisition and dedication to the public of open spaces in or near London"*.

Common land appealed to Octavia Hill because it offered the freedom to roam without the constraints of following a right of way which left *"the narrowest admissible pathway for the public"*. That's just what the grouse moor owners expect the public to settle for today. At that time Octavia Hill wrongly believed that common land was forever safe from cultivation or fencing:

"To walk merely along the roads, if these roads pass between parks or fields barricaded from entrance, frets the human love of freedom which makes us want to wander further, to escape the dusty prescribed track, to break away over the hills, or pause in the meadow by the pool or the river, or gather flowers in the wood. The more these are and must be closed, the more intensely precious does the common or forest, safe for ever from inclosure, become. It is not only the suburban common, it is the rural also which is of value to us as a people."

She also pointed out in her book *Our Common Land*, in 1877, that pressure on commons was not restricted to the area around London, or even those in reach of the railway network which was leading to *"suburb stretching ... beyond suburb as year succeeds year"*:

"And there is a reason why even the still more distant rural commons should if possible be saved from inclosure. Every year, in many country neighbourhoods, population is increasing, and houses for letting are being built; more and more the field-paths by the river-side are being closed, and the walks through the cornfields or bright upland meadows are being shut. The hedge through the many gaps of which it was easy once to step into the roadside-wood and to gather primroses in thousands is now stoutly repaired, and new boards are put up warning trespassers that they 'will be prosecuted'. In self-defence the landowners erect barriers and warn off the public wherever the public becomes numerous."

History can tend to repeat itself, whatever may be said to the contrary. In 1877, Miss Hill joined "*young clergyman*" Hardwicke Drummond Rawnsley in outrage that Manchester's greed and need for water would engulf "*one of our loveliest lakes*" – Thirlmere – in the same way that the brilliant advocate Norman Birkett flung himself into saving its deeper cousin, Ullswater, in the 1960s. Octavia did not have Birkett's measure of success but she had the foresight to realise that even failed agitation "*may help to save other places*".

She argued that the Victorian pursuit of outdoor leisure was making rural commons increasingly important:

"*Now, I hardly know how far out of a large town Bank-holiday excursionists go, but I know they go every year farther and farther. I am sure that a common twelve, nay, twenty miles off from a large town is accessible by cheap trains to hundreds of excursionists all the summer, to whom it is an inestimable boon. Again, is the privilege of space, and light, and air, and beauty not to be considered for the small shop-keeper, for the hard-working clerk, who will probably never own a square yard of English land, but who cares to take his wife and children into the country for a fortnight in the summer? Do you not know numbers of neighbourhoods where woods, and commons, and fields used to be open to pedestrians, and now they must walk, even in the country, on straight roads between hedges? The more that fields and woods are closed, the more does every atom*

11

of common land, everywhere, all over England, become of importance to the people of every class, except that which owns its own parks and woods."

In 1878 the Kyrle Society appointed *"a Committee on Open Spaces"*, with C.E. Maurice as its *"most active and zealous secretary"* to work with the Commons Preservation Society. This committee *"rescued from waste and adorned several churchyards and small but invaluable open spaces"* and led the efforts *"to convert the site of Horsemonger Lane Gaol into a Public Garden, and to make the Gardens of Lincoln's Inn Fields more available to the public"*. On the wider canvas its great achievement was to play *"an important part in bringing about the purchase of Burnham Beeches"*.

Robert Hunter of Meadfields at Haslemere was the honorary solicitor of the Commons Preservation Society from 1868 until the conclusion of its greatest single battle. That was on 6 May 1882 when Epping Forest was not only saved from enclosure but was declared open as a public park by Queen Victoria, in a ceremony at High Beach.

In September 1884, now a vice-president of the society, Hunter addressed the National Association for the Promotion of Social Science, meeting in Birmingham, and outlined the *"three distinct perils"* which were causing widespread losses of common land. Land commissioners were enclosing it. Industrial undertakings, railway companies and local government corporations were appropriating it. Lords of the manor were also carrying out their own enclosures.

"The remedy," he suggested, was *"the formation of a Corporate Company"* to acquire and protect open spaces for the enjoyment of the public.

The Commons Preservation Society published his speech as a threepenny pamphlet, and in response to this Octavia Hill wrote to Hunter in February 1885 with some thoughts on the question of a name for the proposed landowning organisation.

Her suggestion was *"The Commons and Gardens Trust for*

accepting, holding and purchasing open spaces for the people in town and country".

It prompted Hunter to think up something snappier."? *National Trust.*" he pencilled at the top of her letter. It was some question mark.

Another important concept was also launched in 1884. James Bryce MP, chairman of the Commons Preservation Society since 1880 and later to be British Ambassador in Washington, was proposing what is now regarded as the pioneer attempt at giving the open-air movement a basic legal right to enjoy the countryside. His landmark legislation aimed at reinstating ancient rights in Scotland by conferring new liberties on the people in the form of freedom to roam across open country.

The preamble to his Access to Mountains (Scotland) Bill accused landowners of turning wild moorland into game preserves and then preventing public access. These *"large tracts of uncultivated mountain and moor land in Scotland, formerly depastured by sheep and cattle, have of late years been stocked with deer, and attempts have been made to deprive Her Majesty's subjects of the right which they have heretofore enjoyed of walking upon these and other tracts of uncultivated mountain and moor land for purposes of recreation and scientific or artistic study*".

Bryce's 1884 bill proposed that *"no owner or occupier of uncultivated mountain and moor lands in Scotland shall be entitled to exclude any person from walking or being on such land for the purposes of recreation or scientific or artistic study, or to molest him in so walking or being*".

The bill failed to become law, as would a more extensive measure – including England and Wales in its scope – which Charles Trevelyan introduced in 1908. Among those who did vote in favour were two future Prime Ministers, Ramsay MacDonald and Winston Churchill.

Hereon it was Robert Hunter's vision of 1884 that was materialising on the map and on the ground, in the form of representative parcels of generally high-grade scenery that came into the hands of the National Trust. From the beginning the Trust set an example that the politicians have consistently refused to grant as a right, by allowing the public the freedom to roam across uncultivated land. These informal and expanding access opportunities have arguably diffused what might otherwise have become unstoppable pressure for a formal right in law.

"*How to make a Socialist,*" proclaimed Fun magazine of 28 December 1887, above drawings of a yokel staring aghast at notices outside his thatched cottage: "*Knowing he is too poor to go to law – steal his bits of Common and shut him out. Then stop his footpaths.*"

Meanwhile, from 1884, there would be a further decade before Hunter's "*? National Trust*" lost its question mark by becoming incorporated under the Companies Act on 12 January 1895.

The Commons Preservation Society's proceedings for 1885 records Robert Hunter's proposals, before the Social Science Congress, for "*the formation of a company, under the Limited Liability Acts, for the purpose of acquiring and holding land and other property as an aid to the preservation of Commons. The possession by a body friendly to the preservation of open spaces of such properties entitled to Common rights would in many cases prevent encroachments of Commons which at present either pass unchallenged or lead to costly litigation, while it is believed that the management of such properties would be at least self-supporting. At the same time the existence of a corporate body capable of accepting gifts of land and money would tend to facilitate the preservation of open spaces, and to extend the interest felt in the work.*"

The first meeting "*to consider the practicality of the scheme*" to establish a landholding organisation was held at the home of James Bryce, chairman of the society, on 16 February 1885. Representatives of the Commons Preservation Society, the Metropolitan Public Gardens Association and of the Kyrle Society formed a committee from their ranks that held several meetings in 1885 and decided *"to try the experiment of establishing such a company by provisionally opening a share list"* with these being offered at £1.

Shaw-Lefevre resumed the chairmanship of the society from James Bryce later in 1885 and held the post, coupling it with being vice-president, until being created first Baron Eversley in 1904. He was then elected president of the society.

On 15 June 1888, seconding a resolution by Lord Thring, Miss Hill helped persuade the Commons Preservation Society, holding its annual meeting at the palatial Grosvenor House home of its richest committee member, the Duke of Westminster, to extend its campaign to footpaths: *"I am only speaking to you today because it seems to me that a critical time has arrived in which it is incumbent on us all to do what in us lies to preserve for our countrymen and women and their children one of the great common inheritances to which, as English citizens they are born, the footpaths of their native country, through the woods, over the moors, across the fields, by the rivers, and up the hills. As children how we knew them, these little winding, quiet by-ways with all their beauty. Now how they are vanishing. Here, closed by quarter sessions, the poor witnesses hardly daring to speak, the richer dividing the spoil, the public from a larger area hardly knowing of the decision which has for ever closed to them some lovely walk. Then there are the losses of paths boldly closed without legal right by many a high-handed owner, whose neighbours have not knowledge, courage, money, or perseverance to protect the paths which were their common possession. Once lost these paths can never be regained. Let us, before it is too late, unite to preserve them."*

Octavia classed herself among the *"few unknown heroes fighting an uphill fight for a great cause"* and painted the canvas which it is the National Trust's privilege to inherit: *"I think men love a country more when its woods, and fields, and streams, and flowers, and lakes, and hills, and the sky that bends over them are visible. I think men are better for the whisper of their quiet voices when the din of the city ceases, and the time of rest begins. I think these little winding ways, that lead us on by hedgerow and over brooks, through scented meadows, and up grassy hill, away from dusty roads, and into the silent green of wood and field, are a common possession we ought to try to hand down undiminished, in number and in beauty for those who are to follow."*

The Rev. Hardwicke Rawnsley also spoke in Grosvenor House that day. He protested against the attempts at closing a path to the summit of Latrigg in the Lake District. It was also a test-case for Skiddaw. He considered it offensive to have to seek the landowners "*leave*" to go anywhere.

Rawnsley's hopes were a little exaggerated. He thought that the barring of Skiddaw would lead the legislature in Westminster to enact that England was a free country, enabling northern workers access to the hills as of right, he imagined, similar to that enjoyed up "*Welsh and Scotch hills, the more so as there were no grouse or red deer in England.*" Tell that to Sir Anthony Milbank of the Moorland Association or those who drive exhausted hinds on to rocky National Trust land at Holford in Somerset. The National Trust has been abused as the respectable cover for blood sports in England. It cannot assume another century of quiet acquiescence.

Three members of the society, Octavia Hill, Robert Hunter, and Miss Mary Parton, founded the River Wandle Open Spaces Society in the late 1880s to secure "*the preservation of several charming sites on the banks of that, at one time, beautiful stream*". This society handed over its 11 acre holdings at Merton Abbey Wall and Watermeads, facing Ravensbury Park, to the National Trust, in 1913-16. Two acres of the Happy Valley at Mitcham Bridge were given in memory of Octavia Hill in 1915.

The Commons Preservation Society not only had influence but people then knew what it was trying to preserve; not the House of Commons.

J.M. Barrie used the word common as shorthand not only for common land but the countryside as a whole, when he put the writing talents of Thomas Hardy above those of Richard Jeffries, observing in 1889 that Hardy *"knows the common as well as Mr. Jeffries knew it; but he knows the inhabitants as well as the common"*.

Five committee members of the society at that time would not only become remarkable for their longevity but the sustained interest which would see them still serving on that committee into the 1930s. They were Lord Fitzmaurice Pollock [elected 1874], Sir Frederick Pollock [1884], and from the 1888 intake of members Lord Farrer, Lord Olivier and the Rt. Hon. Henry Hobhouse. In October 1889, Octavia Hill found Shaw-Lefevre reluctant to advance the idea for a landowning preservation trust. *"Mr. Shaw-Lefevre does not rise to the idea of the new society,"* she wrote, placing her hopes for its *"head man"* in the society's other prominent spokesman, G.E. Briscoe Eyre.

Octavia Hill continued to link the footpaths cause with that of commons, and was by 1893 putting the paths first: *"It remains the hardest of all things to get either workers or money for the preservation of paths and commons, which are among our people's best possession, and are being yearly, yes, monthly, snatched from them."*

The first meeting to discuss a draft constitution to enable the formation of *"a general trustee for all property intended for the use and enjoyment of the nation at large"* was held at the offices of the Commons Preservation Society, 1 Great College Street, Westminster, on 16 November 1893. It was attended by Walter Besant, Holman Hunt, Professor Huxley, G.F. Watts and, whatever his personal doubts, the society's chairman, George Shaw-Lefevre. They had before them, as a model of legislation, the Trustees of Public Reservations Act passed by the state of Massachusetts in 1891. The meeting decided to apply to the Board of Trade for a licence to establish a non-profit-making joint stock company. The documentation contained several references to the need to secure land *"for public recreation"*. When they founded the National Trust, on 16 July 1894 at the Duke of Westminster's sumptuous Grosvenor House, in Park

Lane, Sir Robert Hunter was not the "*Sir*" of National Trust literature – he was plain Mr; Canon Rawnsley was not that either, he was merely "*the Reverend*". Sir came two decades later for Hunter, and then it would not be for forming the Trust.

Incorporation as a company was formalised in January 1895 and the first secretary of the National Trust was a 22-year-old Australian, Lawrence Wensley Chubb, who would then be secretary of the Commons Preservation Society from 1896 until his death in 1948.

2—Gloucestershire Stile.
A very primitive erection. Stone fences are generally erected instead of hedges on each side.

3—Light Iron Gate.
Self-closing, used at Harrogate, with the words "Public Footpath" on each.

4—Cumberland Stile.
Erected where stone abounds—very permanent.

Saved lands

For Queen Victoria's diamond jubilee in 1897 a special committee was formed by the Commons Preservation Society, the Kyrle Society, the Metropolitan Public Gardens Association and the newly formed National Trust for Places of Historic Interest or Natural Beauty. The society was represented by its chairman Shaw-Lefevre, treasurer Sir John T. Brunner and J.R. Brooke: "*The main objects of the committee were to advocate the provision of open spaces and the preservation of sites of historic interest or natural beauty as a desirable and permanent means of celebrating the 60th year of the reign of Queen Victoria.*" Circulars were sent to every local authority in England and Wales and most in Scotland and Ireland. "*The net result of the committee's operations, as far as can be ascertained, is that over 651 acres of land have been added to the open spaces of the country, the number of successful schemes being 66.*"

The Commons Preservation Society added "*Footpaths*" to its title on merging with the National Footpaths Preservation Society in 1899. It was now the Commons and Footpaths Preservation Society.

The passing of the Devil's Punch Bowl and a 750 acre package of common land at Hindhead, Surrey, into National Trust ownership was only two stages removed from the dramatic courtroom suicide of bankrupt financier Whitaker Wright in 1905. The mortgagees then foreclosed on his loans and put the land to auction. Enclosure was an unlikely threat but the disfigurement caused by gravel digging and heath fires spurred Robert Hunter and Lawrence Chubb to form a Haslemere branch of the Commons and Footpaths Preservation Society. They were pleasantly surprised that it required less than £5 per acre – a total of £3,620 – to secure the land for the National Trust in 1906.

There was also an almost instant home for the spare cash. As the Hindhead Purchase Committee reported to members on its success, news came that Ludshott Common, 542 acres across the

Hampshire border at Bramshott, was being auctioned along with 27 acres of woodland and ponds. This time there was a strong emotive element behind the fund raising – this was Gilbert White country.

Hunter and Chubb came to a private deal with the owner to buy the land for £2,350 and the difference between that and the £1,800 they raised was met by selling ten acres of the wood, beyond Waggoners' Wells, to an adjoining landowner. The remainder of this tract of hilly country was vested in the National Trust and local people continued to contribute land and money, enabling another 90 acres to be added to the Hindhead holdings.

That land includes Gibbet Hill which has been the beneficiary of changing custom with respect to serious offenders. Writing when it was in use, separated from it by just a few feet of air, William Cobbett said this was *"the most villainous spot that God ever made"*.

It and the other lands were now being held *"for the benefit of the nation"* with the bestowing on the Trust of statutory recognition and duties under the National Trust Act of 1907.

There was a little reflected glory for the Commons Preservation Society and its National Trust prodigy in 1911 when one of their mutual leading members, Robert Hunter, the society's honorary solicitor, was rewarded with a knighthood. This honour was not for his campaigning to save open space – he became Sir Robert Hunter in recognition of three decades public service as solicitor to the Post Office. He was in his late sixties and had only two years to live.

After a grand plan to purchase Frensham Great Common as *"the Hunter Memorial"* failed with the Great War, moneys raised as a tribute to Sir Robert Hunter were used to buy Waggoners' Wells for the National Trust in 1919.

Those 14 acres were added to the National Trust's Ludshott Common holding, on the Hampshire-Surrey borderland, which had been secured in the 1908 appeal. Post-war public access was secured at Frensham, in default of ownership, but the War Office also extended its rights: "*Tanks may be used, provided they are not over ten tons in weight.*" To put this in perspective, in 1991 the British Army would plough the sands of the Arabian peninsula with sixty-ton tanks.

In the 1920s the society's chairman, Cecil Harmsworth – Lord Northcliffe's brother – was instrumental in turning the London site of mariner Thomas Coram's original foundling hospital into an open space with a difference. It became a children's playground to which adults are allowed admission only if accompanied by a child.

A partial success for the society was through the intervention of one of its vice-presidents, Lord Buckmaster, who talked Lord Haldane into recommending in 1924 that the Law of Property Bill should have a clause providing for public access for air and exercise to all common lands. Unfortunately the committee's draft was fudged to delete rural commons from this legislation and the wording in the 1925 act restricted the statutory right of access to those commons within the Metropolitan police district or the area of a borough or an urban district council.

Lord Eversley, now as president, marked the society's diamond jubilee in 1925 by launching an appeal fund for the continuation of "*the people's watch dog*" the achievements of which had "*exceeded the most sanguine hopes of the founders of the Society of whom I am now the only survivor. We claim that, through our efforts, over 400,000 acres of land have been saved for the use and enjoyment of the people of this country.*"

Edward North Buxton, a committee member of the society from the late 1860s and a vice-president by the turn of the century, and his elder son Gerald Buxton of Birch Hall, Theydon Bois, were mainly responsible for the rescue of 900 acres of Hatfield Forest and its vesting in the National Trust. That was "*the third Essex forest to be saved largely through the efforts of the Buxton family*". Gerald Buxton's brother, Major Anthony Buxton, was a member of the society's committee, and Gerald's son, Lieutenant-Colonel E.N. Buxton, was its treasurer.

Society secretary Lawrence Chubb seems to have wavered on the cause of the Surrey commons and their defence from the War Department which wanted to turn them into training and firing ranges. Researcher Janet Collett has unearthed a fascinating correspondence and notes of meetings. Chubb had discussed the threat with Sir Herbert Creedy at the War Office on 11 October 1927. He was given no guarantee that areas of common land would not be sold for building. Neither, Creedy admitted, would such assurances and promises that the present Prime Minister might give be binding on his successors.

Despite this, Chubb capitulated on matters of principle and said he would withdraw his opposition if no permanent buildings, new roads or rifle ranges were put on the commons that were acquired. It was agreed that consultation would take place "*as to the nature and scope of manoeuvres ... and the weight of the actual vehicles*". Public access would still be allowed to all the areas in Hampshire and the vicinity of Witley "*unless actually in use for military purposes*". Such activities were to be limited: "*Commons can used for military purposes for two months per year.*"

Chubb thought he had done well: "*Sir Herbert was quite frank and friendly, in view of the fact that the War Office have found it necessary to accept the views of the Commons Preservation Society as regards Lulworth Cove and in various other disputes which have arisen since the Great War.*"

Rights owner Herbert Binnie expressed disappointment: "*For it would seem that you have lost heart in the fight, and you are thinking of making a strategic retreat, just as the real fight is on. This is surely not the person who told me some little while back, he was prepared to fight to the last against acquisition, and would even try to get someone to buy the commons and present them to the National Trust to prevent it.*"

Chubb's reticence may not have been entirely unrelated to the fact that he would soon be receiving a knighthood.

Earl Russell, however, pressed for answers in the House of

Lords: "*There is a feeling that the attitude of the War Office is like the attitude of the wolf to Red Riding Hood. People who use and live near the commons are afraid that the commons may be swallowed up and cease to be available for purposes of public recreation.*"

Something was achieved, for the deeds of some 2,200 acres were exchanged between Richard Coombe and Herbert Binnie – owners of manorial rights in Frensham, Thursley, Hankley, and part of Witley parishes – and Chubb who acted on behalf of the society: "*The deeds have been executed under section 193 of the Law of Property Act, 1925, to give the public a statutory right of access to the commons for air and exercise.*"

That said, the society reported in the first issue of its journal, there were already 13,000 acres of common land that were in the possession of the military authorities. Sir Lawrence Chubb was the joint secretary of the special Purchase Committee which for twelve years, under the umbrella of the society, worked to raise a total of £12,500 for the purchase of the 199 acre Selsdon Wood in Surrey. This he then vested in the National Trust, leaving its future management to a joint committee of the Trust and the Croydon, Coulsdon, and Purley local authorities.

That was in 1935 but the story started with plans for immediate housing development in 1924. Chubb himself had purchased an important stretch of road frontage, largely to ensure the survival of a great patch of herb paris, which has in Somerset the more romantic name of true-lovers' knot. It is "*fit to be nourished in every good Woman's garden,*" Culpepper wrote.

The original 925 acres of what are now the Bramshaw Commons group of holdings, along the northern edge of the New Forest, was given to the National Trust by the widow of society member G.E. Briscoe Eyre in 1923-30. The land included Cadnam and Plaitford commons.

On the western side of the New Forest, on the brow of the hill where the A31 drops down to Ringwood, members of the society raised the money to buy 30 acres Hightown Common and present it to the Trust in 1929 in memory of Lord Eversley, who as George Shaw-Lefevre had founded the Commons Preservation society in 1865.

The appeal fund for Hightown Common included provision for the erection of "*a monolith, fountain or shelter*" in memory of Lord Eversley. In the event it was a monumental wayside seat.

In teak and Purbeck stone, this was designed by Miss Elisabeth Scott, the architect of the Shakespeare Memorial Theatre.

Cecil Harmsworth, chairman of the society, made the presentation of the deeds there on 28 May 1931, with Sir Harry Stephen accepting them on behalf of the National Trust. They paid tribute to Lord Eversley's great campaign to save the 16,000 acres of commons in and around London, but he also had a direct interest in little Hightown Common, having urged the society's secretary, Sir Lawrence Chubb, to secure its preservation. That discussion took place only a fortnight before Lord Eversley's death.

The acquisition of Hightown Common had its origins in a defence committee, instigated by Tom Longstaff, Major Colin Ziegler and Dr. Beddard. Forty acres had been offered for sale as common grazing land on the disposal of the Ringwood part of the Morant Estate, in 1916, but remained unsold until the mid-1920s, when it was acquired by W.J. Ayles who built a brick-kiln and started to dig for clay, sand and gravel. Counsel's opinion failed to frighten him off but eventually he settled for £800 for the land and £100 to demolish his kiln and drying shed.

The Commons and Footpaths Preservation Society added "*Open Spaces*" to its title, ignoring warnings that the name was "*becoming unduly long*", at its annual general meeting on 30 April 1928. It was now the Commons, Open Spaces and Footpaths Preservation Society. That name was eventually proposed by Miss Dorothy Hunter after H.J. Tozer and others had resisted an attempt by Sir Edgar Bonham Carter and Randolph A. Glen to delete "*Preservation*" from the society's title.

Two long-standing members of the society, A. Bray and

Beresford Heaton, resolved *"some differences of opinion with regard to the ownership of a salient feature of Hackhurst Down"* at Shere, Surrey, by conveying the 13 acres to the National Trust in 1928. *"The gift will be widely appreciated as Hackhurst Downs are one of the finest view-points of Surrey,"* the society's journal proclaimed.

Littleheath Wood, 52 acres of land between Selsdon and South Croydon, was bought through a £6,000 appeal raised by Malcolm Sharpe, the treasurer of the society's Kent and Surrey Committee, in 1929: *"Littleheath Wood is a charming tract containing many fine timber trees. That the scheme has not been launched a moment too soon is proved by the fact that whole streets of new houses have lately been erected right up to the area which it is proposed to acquire."*

The society's chairman in the 1920s and '30s, Cecil Harmsworth, presented Dr. Samuel Johnson's house in Gough Square to the nation in 1929. It was where the great dictionary was compiled. To sample its entries, begin with oats: *"A grain which in England is generally given to horses, but in Scotland supports the people."*

Knighton Woods, 40 acres of the Knighton Estate at Buckhurst Hill, Essex, was bought in 1930 as a result of a public appeal in memory of Edward North Buxton, who, as one of the original committee members of the society and long-time vice-president, had already left his mark on the landscape of Essex in London by saving much of Epping and Hainault Forests.

Little Hampden Common, 50 acres of the most attractive part of Buckinghamshire, was formerly known as Hampden Green, and could be traced back through the court rolls for over 450 years, but in 1928 Captain Trevor Battye put fences around it to prevent *"the habit of driving at will over the land, of lighting fire, and of breaking down shrubs and undergrowth"*. Protest meetings were held and the fences torn down. Rather than embark on litigation, however, the society approached the owner and offered to buy his rights on the independent valuation of Sir

Howard Frank, to vest the land in the National Trust. In the event, in 1930, the owner instead made a revocable access deed under section 193 of the Law of Property Act, 1925.

The society has from its inception monitored the decisions of the courts and drawn them to the attention of interested members. To quote one such:

"Strolling about a wood for courting purposes is not a right known to the common law, whether by way of profit a prendre or otherwise," His Honour Judge Barnard Lailey pronounced in 1930.

On the North Downs in Surrey the society's local branch, the Reigate and Redhill Open Spaces and Footpaths Preservation Society, launched a £3,500 appeal in 1931 to buy nine acres of Reigate Hill which would otherwise *"inevitably pass into the hands of the builders"*. Several more pieces would follow there and around Box Hill. Post-war reinstatement of the Pilgrims Way across the River Mole, below Box Hill, would be the zenith of the Open Spaces Society in terms of political influence, with the replacement stepping stones of wartime tank-trap concrete being provided at the personal expense of Home Secretary and society member James Chuter-Ede in 1946 and declared open by Prime Minster Clement Attlee. At the celebratory dinner that followed, the Lord Mayor of London proposed the toast to *"The Commons, Open Spaces and Footpaths Preservation Society,"* and the Prime Minster replied.

Poor's Acre, in fact 18 acres of roadside grass and hilltop trees in the middle of Haugh Wood, near Woolhope, Herefordshire, was acquired by the National Trust in 1931 through the society. *"It lies high and is said to have the most beautiful and varied views in the county,"* the Trust reported in 1932. *"Previously vested in Fawnhope Parish Council which sold it to the Forestry Commissioners. Now bought back through the Commons Open Spaces and Footpaths Preservation Society and handed over to the National Trust."*

By 1932, 126 acres of Selsdon Wood *"within easy walking*

distance of Croydon" had been saved by the society's Purchase Committee "*as a nature reserve and bird sanctuary*" for £3,450. The appeal moved on to raise the same again twice over to purchase the adjoining 42 acres of Hillocks Wood and 31 acres down by the Old Farleigh Road, which "*with the advantage of a water supply*" was under the greatest pressure from development.

In 1932-34 the society saved Cornwall's Lizard Common, 70 acres spreading three-quarters of a mile from Kynance towards the Lizard, for the National Trust. In 1932, society members Stenton Covington and A.T. Cummings donated £100 which was paid to the Ministry of Agriculture for the carrying out of a regulation scheme. They then talked the owners into "*vesting the soil*" of the common with the Trust. Its "*remarkable cliff scenery*" includes the offshore Lion Rock, a dramatic Victorian painting of which by J.H.J. Millar now hangs above the writer's desk.

In 1933, all of Selsdon Wood was safe, though as yet unfenced. That would require £2,000, bringing the total cost of the 199 acres to £13,000 – £65 per acre – for securing "*the largest and most beautiful open space acquired for many years in the south of the Metropolitan area*". It was reported that "*the National Trust has agreed to accept the guardianship of the wood if it can be assured of an income of £150 per annum*". One presumes it was.

Whether land acquired through the society went to the National Trust or other sympathetic owners depended largely upon whether the former already had a management presence in the locality. In 1934, for instance, by means of a loan from the Pilgrim Trust the society in turn loaned Lymington Borough Council the money to purchase 41 acres of open clifftop heathland at Barton Common which was and is separated by the New Forest from the nearest National Trust lands.

At the same time, the society in London and Miss Clarke-Williams in Storrington, Sussex, raised the £1,740 to save 29 acres of the Weald at Sullington Warren with its double line of prehistoric burial mounds, *"from building development"*. This land was given to the National Trust.

In Berkshire .the society encouraged residents to buy the Manor of Cookham and Maidenhead for the Trust in 1934. Several of its eight parcels of land are extensive and together they cover 843 acres.

Mow Cop Castle, a romantic ruin of 1750 at 1,091 feet on the Cheshire-Staffordshire border, where the first meeting of the Primitive Methodists took place in 1807, came into National Trust ownership following the society's intervention in 1935. The folly was offered as a gift by Joseph Lovatt but the Trust required that first it was put into a safe condition. The society launched a £400 restoration fund and also persuaded Mr. Lovatt to grant the public unrestricted access rights across the adjoining eight acres.

Expressing delight in 1935 that several hilltops had been given to the National Trust, the society issued a reminder that hills are not only places of pilgrimage for the living but the traditional burial places of northern European cultures. Both aspects could be promoted, for the benefit of the landscape and the public, by a renaissance of English landed eccentricism: *"No memorial is so enduring as a hill, and a member of the society makes the suggestion that landowners whose territory includes some noble or lovely summit should give directions in their wills for their remains to be interred there, with what monument or epitaph, simple or elaborate, they desire, and for the hill and a means of access to it to be given to the public. Such a benefaction would endure while the earth remains and would give lasting enjoyment to many, and we commend the suggestion to all those among our readers who could adopt it for themselves."*

In 1936 Chubb was at it again. He launched a £1,100 appeal to buy the 116 acre open space of Hudnall Common beside Whipsnade Zoo in Hertfordshire. He had already saved a woodland walk at Ashbridge and the stocks at Alderbury. There the society had secured a legal victory nearly seventy years before when it safeguarded the collective lands known as Berkhamsted Common.

Moving out of the Home Counties in 1936, the society started the successful campaign to extend the group of National Trust properties near Stroud, Gloucestershire. It resulted in the acquisition of Rodborough Common which covers 242 acres and had been threatened by ploughing.

When the Reigate and Redhill branch of the society handed over two pieces of land, of eight acres and two-and-a-quarter acres, to the National Trust, the point was made that their importance was not to be reckoned in terms of size as they were crucial chains in the "*Green Belt*". These particular links were at Margery Wood and Reigate Hill.

Also that year and in Surrey, society member Miss Ballantine Dykes bought 20 acres of disputed common land, arguably part of Blackheath Common, and presented it to the National Trust. With a new National Trust Act in 1937 its purpose was extended to "*the promotion of access ... to its properties*".

The Hudnall Common appeal was successfully concluded in 1938, just a few pounds short of its target, with the society making up the difference from its own funds so that the land could be conveyed to the National Trust.

Between 1897 and the Second World War the Commons, Open Spaces and Footpaths Preservation Society had been the catalyst if not the actual paymaster in securing permanent public access through freehold purchases to some 8,000 acres of open space and woodland, most of which had been under threat.

Of that acreage, the bulk was handed to the National Trust, where the memory of common ground between the organisations – and indeed the story of how members of the society founded the Trust – inevitably faded into folklore and obscurity. I estimate that 5,000 acres, which is nearly eight square miles, came to the Trust through the direct efforts of society and its members.

By 1990 that had been so utterly forgotten that the initial question I received over lunch preceding my first meeting of the

Trust's ruling council queried my credentials as chairman of the Open Spaces Society, which is what the Commons, Open Spaces and Footpaths Preservation Society now calls itself: "*Isn't the National Trust rather on the fringes for you in the allotments movement?*" This provoked and inspired me to research the common roots between the two organisations and then to comment on how at that time the Trust seemed in danger of allowing countryside access to be eclipsed by its latter-day role as the guardian and safety-net for country house estates.

Others on the Trust's council were aware of the Society's work. Sir John Smith encouraged our initiative in seeking to register new village greens. The incoming chairman, Lord Chorley, told me of his father's presidency of the Commons Preservation Society from 1961 until 1975.

5—Bachelor's Gate.
Very convenient. Swinging part about 4 feet high by 3 feet wide.

6—Turnstile.
Objectionable. Soon gets out of order by children riding on it.

30

Lost commons
Public understanding of just what is common land, let alone any comprehension of its complex thousand years of custom and law, is now at its lowest ebb and indeed comparable with the level of interest shown in allotments. If commons are seen as anything it is for what they are not – as the people's land.

Legislation has never risen to meet the public conception but may be expected to do so in the future.

The twentieth century was the high-water mark of losses on all fronts, with upwards of 1,500,000 acres being reduced to below 1,300,000 acres by failures to claim parcels of land under the Commons Registration Act of 1965. Not that I accept the oft-quoted 1,500,000-acre estimate which has its origins in a Victorian report of the Local Government Board. At about the same time, in 1874, the Inclosure Commissioners said 2,600,000 acres of common land remained unenclosed. Their statement is probably more authoritative and a compromise midway between the two figures would give upwards of two million acres which is consistent with the substantial attrition rate which climaxed in the post-1965 loss of commons caused by non-registration – which extended also to village greens where even the Archers of Ambridge failed to register theirs. Then came deregistrations, though as steady drips rather than a haemorrhage. Second-stage protective laws have still failed to materialise and it is unlikely to be before the twenty-first century that there is a proper mechanism for cherishing what is still a rich heritage and the last major vestige of mediaeval land usage.

This generation of politicians have ducked their chance and evaded what became a momentary manifesto commitment aimed at seducing the green vote. The nineteenth century still offers the inspiration that we can do better.

The National Trust has done a relatively good job in gathering common land in its property portfolio, to the extent of 160,000 acres which is 28 per cent of its 580,000 acres, but this is less than 13 per cent of the total acreage of commons in England and

31

Wales. It is unrealistic to expect the Trust to do more than protect a representative spread of such lands and to give future emphasis to the acquisition of the striking and the glamorous rather than the fragmented and the neglected in ordinary landscape.

Much of its common land came either through the Commons Protection Society or because of the heightened awareness that the society was able to engender in others. They and the politicians were closer to the historic roots of common land and understood its potential contribution to what, paraphrasing Octavia Hill, were the *"open air sitting rooms for the poor"*.

Such space was already at a premium. That it was endangered would concentrate Octavia's mind but, as she was well aware, common land in particular had been under threat since time immemorial.

Shakespeare, writing *Henry VI* in about 1590, mentions a petition *"Against the Duke of Suffolk, for enclosing the commons of Melford."* The petitioner responds: *"Alas, sir! I am but a poor petitioner of our whole township."*

Therapeutic moral values were seen in country walking by the seventeenth century parson and poet George Herbert of Bemerton, Wiltshire. He regarded rogationtide ceremonies, in which the Church continued pagan practices of beating the bounds, as more than a means of ensuring the integrity and preservation of boundaries. Leading his flock around the edge of the parish was also an exercise in practical spirituality, thought the rector who set them the example of a saint: *"Charitie, in loving walking and neighbourly accompanying one another, with reconciling of differences at that time, if they be any."*

The nymphs and shepherds of Michael Drayton's pastoral epic poem *Poly-Olbion* have their contemporary reality in a letter from Dorothy Osborne to her lover, Sir William Temple, in May 1653. It was very much the merry month at Chicksands in Bedfordshire: *"The heat of the day is spent in reading or working, and about six or seven o'clock I walk out into a common that lies hard by the house, where a great many young wenches keep sheep and cows, and sit in the shade singing of ballads. I go to them and compare their voices and beauties to some ancient shepherdesses I have read of, and find a vast difference there; but, trust me, I think these are as innocent as could be."*

When Oliver Goldsmith wrote *The Deserted Village*, in 1768-70, the extent of common land in England and Wales had declined to less than half of the estimated seven million acres that existed in the time of Queen Anne.

The Queen herself attempted to purloin a famous London open space. *"Were I to enclose Green Park within my garden, what would be the cost?"* Queen Anne asked her chief minister.

"A monarchy, Madam. A monarchy," Sidney Godolphin replied.

Mediaeval open fields were being turned into England's patchwork quilt of hedgerows as the urge to enclose became unstoppable all across the country:

*"Fenceless fields the sons of wealth divide
and e'en the bare worn common is denied."*

William Cobbett jibbed at the use of the legal term "*waste*" to describe open space. He gave as an example, in 1785, Horton Heath in Dorset: *"Wastes indeed! Give a dog an ill name. Was Horton Heath a waste? Was it a 'waste' when a hundred, perhaps, of healthy boys and girls were playing there of a Sunday, instead of creeping about covered with filth in the alleys of a town?"*

Beside it, beneath an ash tree, the fugitive Duke of Monmouth had been captured after the Battle of Sedgemoor, in 1685. The heath's own epitaph would be heard in the House of Lords in 1981, bulldozing having preceded implementation of the Wildlife and Countryside Act which, the owner feared, would tighten the controls on its status as a site of special scientific interest.

The village green had become by the eighteenth century the epitome not just of the rural idyll but of the other figment of the romantic imagination that childhood provides the best days of one's life. The two ideas came together with William Blake:

33

> "*Such, such were the joys*
> *When we all girls and boys*
> *In our youth were seen*
> *On the echoing green."*

Tennyson repeated the image:
> "*Maud with her exquisite face.*
> *And wild voice pealing up to the sunny sky,*
> *And feet like sunny gems on an English green."*

His Maud has her tearful moments, but they are located at the village church, where it is an angel that weeps over her – "*carved in stone*".

There was to be a continuing sense of outrage at the loss of commons, put bitterly and brilliantly by the unknown writer of an epigram that appeared in the Tickler Magazine of 1 February 1821:
> "*The fault is great in man or woman*
> *Who steals a goose from off a common;*
> *But who can plead that man's excuse*
> *Who steals the common from the goose?*"

Whether or not he had found an earlier source, Lord Farrer used to give meetings of the Commons Preservation Society a version that was subtly different:
> "*The Law declares a man a felon*
> *Who steals the goose from off the common*
> *But leaves the greater villain loose*
> *Who steals the common from the goose.*"

The Victorian geologist Hugh Miller was born in Cromarty and at his happiest exploring open country searching out quarries and fossils. When he first came down from the Highlands to Edinburgh, in 1824, he missed the freedom of his native open land:

"*I threw myself, as usual, for compensatory pleasures, on my evening walks, but found the inclosed state of the district, and the fence of a rigorously-administered trespass-law, serious drawbacks; and ceased to wonder that a thoroughly cultivated country is, in most instances, so much less beloved by its people than a wild and open one. Rights of proprietorship may exist equally in both; but there is an important sense in which the open country belongs to the proprietors and to the people too."*

In England it was too late to save urban open space for the major cities of the industrial revolution. *"If the people of Manchester want to go out on Sunday where must they go?"* it was asked in the 1840s. *"There are no public promenades, no avenues, no public gardens, and no public common."*

Opium addicts did not find their vision of England greened by the drug. Its environmental selectivity was to induce dreams of architecture rather than landscape and to start there with cathedrals and towers and descend with time into prisons and dungeons. In *Rambles Beyond Railways*, published in 1851, Wilkie Collins produced the ultimate travelogue of the mind, where sunny Cornwall of the visitor is interspersed with pockets of sadness he had heard about en route between the glorious vistas. He tells of ten frozen fishermen – washed ashore with icicles, on an arctic morning in 1846 – and of the hermit sisters of Tintagel, one of whom died with the survivor then going into a hunger strike of weeping in which she also died a few weeks later.

Yet stronger stuff, from the influence of *"a little of last night's laudanum,"* appears in the novel *Armadale*, published in 1866, where Collins hauntingly describes a woodside setting in Norfolk, besides The Broads. *"The long grazing-grounds rose over its farther shore, with the mist thickening on them, and a dim black line far away of cattle in slow procession going home ..."* It is quintessentially common land England and its impact is underscored by his female character's next lines:

"The place made an unaccountably vivid impression on me, and I can't help writing about it. If I end badly – suppose we say on the scaffold? – I believe the last thing I shall see, before the hangman pulls the drop, will be the little shining pool, and the long misty grazing ground, and the cattle winding dimly home in the thickening night."

That twilight vision of cattle plodding home is as precious and endangered as the *"grazing-grounds"* themselves.

Insidious changes

Encroachments and legal losses are not the only threats to our remaining commons. There is a much more insidious disease that rots their very character. For during the twentieth century, much of the remaining common land in lowland England has ceased to be grazed. Even where stock is still turned out it is usually on a scale that is modest compared with the grazing regimes of the Middle Ages. Other rights have also generally lapsed into obscurity.

Consequently many commons – including a high proportion of those in Trust ownership – are changing in character. Instead of being predominantly open expanses of rough grassland or heath they are becoming smothered in bracken and scrub that in time develops into impenetrable woodland.

This is detrimental to their landscape value in several ways. Firstly it makes them visually indistinguishable from other unkempt woodlands. Secondly it compromises their significance as the last remnants of mediaeval farming systems. Thirdly it is often accompanied by the smothering of actual archaeological remains. Fourthly it degrades their wildlife status. Fifthly it minimises their public access potential by making it physically impossible to walk freely across them in the traditional way.

The National Trust should set a lead in keeping its commons as representative as possible of their original appearance and habitat. This will probably be impossible in the case of many smaller or fragmented examples, so the first priority should be given to those blocks of land that are large enough to be viably stocked for conservation grazing, aided by scrub clearance.

Active intervention of a long-term nature is essential to achieve meaningful improvements, or even to hold the status quo, but it is rendered impossible on unenclosed land if it is not combined with steps to prevent the straying of stock. Perimeter fencing is necessary to keep animals on the Trust's land. Roadside fencing will also be needed wherever traffic levels or speeds lead to the danger of accidents. These are unacceptable for reasons of animal welfare and human safety alike, and soon cause farmers to withdraw their herds.

Such fencing can be contentious. The Trust should proclaim its need as the prerequisite for preserving open landscapes as well as the obvious safety factors. It needs, however, to be located with sensitivity. Positioning at a roadside will avoid the developing of scrub to block the view from the carriageway. It must always be accompanied by stiles or, preferably, gates, at all customary entry points.

Internal fencing has to be resisted. Where essential it can only be of a temporary nature. The aim should be to preserve the open aspect of common land, both for users and as a component of the landscape.

Where the view from the road is of considerable importance it may be possible to devise a stock-holding boundary that is unobtrusive. The ha-ha type of ditch is an example of an invisible barrier.

Just how much of the Trust's common land holdings can be safeguarded by grazing is difficult to calculate. Perhaps only half is in units sizable enough to warrant special schemes or measures. Where it can be done, however, something should be attempted to preserve these holdings as examples of living history. Many are well inside the London commuter belt, where they have become increasingly important with the general degradation of much of the surrounding countryside. Their location tells the story of the germination and evolution of the National Trust.

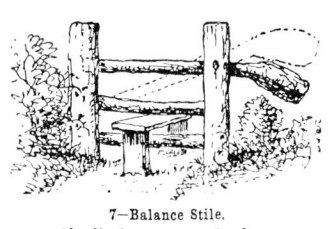

7—Balance Stile.
Also liable to get out of order as No. 6.

8—Step Stile.
Most convenient, and excellent. Also gives seats.

37

Landscape degradation

The Victorian need was for access within reach of the southern conurbations and the industrial cities where the general population could enjoy and experience the countryside for therapeutic and spiritual invigoration. What the National Trust brought for the first time was a reassurance that parcels and pockets of this and the wider landscape would be preserved in perpetuity for and on behalf of the people.

The Trust then looked to fields rather than estates, and to individual buildings rather than whole villages, seeing them as if they were details from a painting or lines from the poem. The countryside was still an integral part of the romantic imagination. Indeed there was no need to endeavour to safeguard the surrounding landscape for that provided a complementary background to the first Trust properties and could be seen as part of the same vision rather than a potential intrusion.

That was particularly the case in terms of wildlife. There was no reason to compile species lists for Trust lands at a time when almost every field in the country would have its seasonal riot of colour, be deluged with butterflies, and have hedgerows rustling with small mammals and resonant with bird song.

Only with Second World War ploughing and the Cold War agricultural revolution, when such areas were systematically reduced to semi-viable oases, did nature reserves need to exist.

Hereon the details mattered and the Trust started to address specifics and diversify into specialities.

Mechanisation and subsidies brought change at a pace to which the Trust found itself at times impossible to resist on its own properties let alone counter in the greater countryside. In *A Guide to Wicken Fen*, the 1947 edition, the Trust states: "*In 1941 the stringency of the nation's food situation forced upon us the unwelcome necessity of allowing Adventurer's Fen to be drained and cultivated by the County War Agricultural Committee. Something of the troubles and enthusiasms of the farmers engaged upon the reclamation can be read in Mr. A. Bloom's book* The Farm in the Fen. *This operation involved complete reorganisation and reconstruction of the system of drainage ditches and an immense amount of expense and labour in the removal of gigantic bog oaks."*

In the process they caused the extinction of the last British sub-species of the large copper butterfly.

Similarly, in the heartlands of Wiltshire, the interior of the Trust-owned Iron Age hill-fort of Figsbury Rings was put under the plough, with consequent damage to the sub-surface archaeology and the destruction of most of its orchid-rich flora.

These examples would eventually be rectified, or at least as best as one ever can put back the clock, but for some 45 per cent of the Trust's total holdings – a total of 260,000 acres of what I called *"ordinary decent farmland"* in a talk in 1990 – the management of the landscape is out of the Trust's direct control. Agricultural tenancy legislation renders the Trust largely impotent to look after almost half of its land. Such changes as have been achieved, as at Manor Farm, Studland, Dorset, and Sherborne Farm, Gloucestershire, have taken place when the land has come back into Trust hands after tenancies have been surrendered.

In these cases opportunities have been grasped to take sensitive areas out of the rented areas, enabling them to be devoted to conservation, public access or landscape enhancement. In the instance of Sherborne Farm there has been the reinstatement of water-meadows under a Countryside Stewardship scheme and a refinement on the usual types of inducement to tenant co-operation. In the past rent reductions have been the carrot for providing public access or conservation management, but at Sherborne the Trust has set a proper market rent without such allowances. Instead payments will be made for the tenant's conservation management as such external contracts are seen as being more easily enforced than the achieving of specific performance for having lowered the rent.

David Bett, the director of the Trust's Wessex region, takes issue with my views on tenanted land and points out that it is *"misleading"* for me to claim that the Trust has no effective control of its farmlands:

"You are quite right that 1948 Agricultural Holdings Act gave tenants extensive freedom over the cropping of their holdings – and the arable acreage had been much extended by the War Agricultural Committees – but landlords are in a position to resist the ploughing up of remaining pastures, the removal of hedges and the demolition of traditional buildings. Most agreements reserve hedgerow trees to the landlord. You can usually identify the National Trust's estates by the density of these remaining features.

"Modern agriculture has taken a terrible toll of traditional farmland flora and fauna but I was struck by the number of conservation (and access) clauses contained in the Trust's coastal farm agreements when I joined the Trust in Devon nearly 25 years ago. Agents have taken every opportunity to improve on old agreements or those inherited from previous owners."

The current Countryside Stewardship scheme is one notch better than the average phoney conservation subsidy that achieves little more than the legalised ripping-off of the Euro-taxpayer. My venom is reserved for the five-year set-asides that are to turn arable land into herb-rich meadows. By the time that worthy objective is achieved the farmers will be able to plough them up again.

In talking of its vast acreages, the Trust should refrain from the boast that it is Britain's biggest *"private"* landowner. It is wrong in fact – the Trust has Acts of Parliament that establish its unique place in the public domain – and it creates an impression that the Trust cherishes an exclusivity distanced from the general population. People on an urban omnibus are unlikely to understand the nuances behind such expressions from Trust officers and staff.

Put bluntly, people do not give legacies to private bodies – it is therefore potentially harmful as well as being wrong. If, on the other hand, the word *"public"* is also unacceptable, implying the Trust is no more than a collection of open access commons, then perhaps *"independent"* is the neutral alternative. Almost anything would be better than that ugly term *"non-governmental"*.

Paths or Allemansratt?

Where National Trust ownership has perhaps distorted the extent of lawful public access is that it has provided a plethora of country houses, parkland, viewpoints, and coastal scenery within a close distance of London. This has diffused what otherwise might have been irresistible pressure for a right to roam – given that until recent times much of the public path network has been unfindable on the ground, if not actually obstructed.

There would also have been pressure for national parks in lowland England, within day-trip distance of London, where obvious examples would be the Chiltern Hills in Oxfordshire, the South Downs in Sussex, and the New Forest in Hampshire. Likewise the Isle of Purbeck, Dorset, was once seriously considered.

Instead, since the Second World War, it has been land owned by the Ministry of Defence that has reverted to primaeval landscape with reservoirs of wildlife. The gems are the splendid military ecology of the Salisbury Plain artillery ranges, Wiltshire, and the Lulworth tank gunnery ranges, Dorset.

Virtual zero-management, with low-intensity rough grazing, has recreated (rather than the recreational "*recreating*" of Countryside Commission jargon) wild landscapes that are self-sustaining and on a scale that amounts to the largest restoration of natural scenery since the downward slide that started with the advent of Neolithic farming in 4,500 BC.

There is potential for the National Trust to do something similar in the twenty-first century. By then, one hopes and anticipates, the next major cause of celebration will be acquisition of its millionth acre. Given the extrapolation of national and European trends there will be scope for taking Trust farmland out of food production, moving by stages as tenants retire or die and land falls back into Trust control.

Why should the National Trust merely preserve and encapsulate vestiges of relict scenery and habitats? I believe it is possible to go much further and create new nature reserves and landscapes.

As a micro-example, on 24 June 1993 when we drew out of

Grateley railway station, Hampshire, I pointed out an expanse of flowering blue cornflowers to David Bett. He was duly impressed at the profusion of such a rarity. The reason for its reappearance was that the recent platform extension, on the west side of the car-park, had disturbed a layer of buried Victorian seed. The landscape of Richard Jeffries and Thomas Hardy lived again, if only for 1993.

Farmers, as the National Trust has started to learn, can be persuaded – money is their only language – into being landscape gardeners. Let their example be George Hastings of Rainthorpe Hall in Norfolk's Tas valley. His is set-aside of lasting merit. A soggy meadow is now a lake with three islands, visited by grass snakes as well as birds. "*They swim,*" he explained, about one of the former. "*Don't worry, it is harmless and doesn't bite!*"

If that is a benefit of the Common Agricultural Policy then I am delighted but the failure of Margaret Thatcher's regime was that it only began to start abolishing subsidies. By 1991 every cow in Europe, including the British one, was costing taxpayers £184 in subsidy payments. I wonder whether it is ethical to subsidise farmers rather than shipbuilders, particularly as the latter have twice gained us an empire though both Elizabethan and Victorian pinks (the colour of ownership) are now equally wiped from the map.

The situation in the Lake District is becoming an economic farce and a landscape disaster. Not only do Lakeland sheep represent £35 a head in subsidy payments, in 1993, but they are clearly reverting into feral animals. Stocking levels of the high commons have doubled in the past decade – to take advantage of subsidies – and conspicuous path erosion on the fells is now being largely caused by over-grazing and flock movements, accentuated and exaggerated by the evolution of non-handled Herdwicks that tend to retreat from walkers far more than their predecessors would have done.

Many of these flocks now have no economic purpose, beyond being paper entries for the purposes of subsidy applications.

They are no longer being being shorn, dipped or tended in any way, they are not culled for meat, and neither are many of the lambs removed from the fells. If the climate were drier up there they would be creating as desert.

None of this is compatible with landscape conservation any more than it makes sense for the European taxpayers. Rents are also falling and there is now a case for the Trust to start regarding farming, even of the so-called traditional type, as a costly and damaging activity that cannot be regarded as sustainable. If it makes no return to the Trust's budget, beyond paying for its administration and the maintenance costs incurred in its upkeep, then farming is a land use that is no longer tenable.

This merely mirrors just what has happened with other forms of holdings as management practises have evolved. Trust-owned woodlands are no longer managed for forestry. Trust-owned lakes and rivers are not managed as commercial fisheries. Neither, I now contend, should farms be managed for commercial agriculture.

Doing just that has, in the past, led to Trust-financed blots on the landscape. In providing factory-sized buildings, coupled with inevitable rent increases, the Trust caused some of its estate farmers to increase the size of their fields by removing hedgerows, triple the use of nitrates, and create slurry lakes. Such abuses and embarrassments must never again be allowed to mar the Trust's record; not all of the horrors of the agricultural revolution can be blamed on governments and subsidies.

Sometimes there has been benefit from the post-war moneys. Subsidies plus import controls have prevented a repeat of the great agricultural depression of 1870 through to 1914 but they have victimised the Third World by preventing market forces from bringing about fair and genuine international prices.

At home it has been an abuse of subsidies and Countryside Commission grants to pay farmers in order to ensure that they do things they should be doing anyway by law, such as reinstating public paths and not destroying scheduled ancient monuments.

Everywhere vernacular agricultural architecture is under threat. Even the National Trust has demolished the quaint Rookery Stalls cowsheds and stables behind the Elizabethan Montacute House in Somerset. They had reduced it by July 1991 to such a state that three of its ruined walls were used as jumps in the Montacute Horse Trials. Elsewhere there was already a change of heart. Prosaic buildings are now in vogue for special conservation reports and the same will soon apply to those surviving pillboxes and other war-works of 1940-44 that avoided being blown up as "*eyesores*" courtesy the Royal Engineers and the conivance of National Trust wardens, as recently as 1988. That incident, from the Purbeck coast, is hearsay, but I did know the underground bunker on the top of Thorncombe Beacon – 508 feet above Lyme Bay – which I stumbled into in childhood and found to be alive with toads. It was still there in the late 1960s, after the land had been given to the Trust by the playwright Robert Cedric Sherriff, but was restored to grass when I returned two decades later. Coastal erosion cannot be the excuse as the concrete war-work was holding the clifftop together rather than forcing it apart.

Attitudes have, however, changed fast. In 1993 the Royal Observer Corps abandoned an underground radiation monitoring post, a relic of the Cold War, to Trust ownership in Upper Wharfedale, Yorkshire. It lies beside a lane beneath Buckden Pike. I was able to argue that it should be preserved as a prospective future ancient monument and that it might even have a use, as a high-security storage facility for the equipment of pot-holers, who are active in the Dales and would be quite at home venturing down its iron ladder.

Here, above ground in Wharfedale, the Trust has a mammoth task in repairing, re-roofing, and at times rebuilding, more than a hundred disused haybarns that are such an integral part of a unique landscape of little stone-walled meadows. Most date only from the mid-nineteenth century, and many on non-Trust land are falling into decay. Arguably, they are becoming romantic ruins, as have castles and abbeys before them, but others see decaying agricultural stonework as a visual obscenity.

Almost as bad is the yuppification of the 1980s and onwards, that part as yet un-named as a lifestyle, which have transformed rustic scenes out of all recognition. Unfortunately is is far more than satellite dishes and security alarms. Far from Trust land, Kate Ashbrook and Chris Hall have shown me deplorable abuses among the barn conversions of the Chilterns. Similarly, also in chalkland, one delightful brick and tile building in a valley near Winfrith, Dorset, had a cottage at one end and an integral big barn at the other.

It is now a superb country house, with floor to roof windows, about as desirable as you could hope for but it has lost all vestiges of its origins and history in the process.

Such restorations are not just unsympathetic: they inflict the disease of sameness from one end of the country to the other.

They also generate insider-hostility to the whole purpose of the countryside. Incomers complain about farm activities and smells, taking their protests to public inquiries as at Trent in Dorset.

They are intolerant of walkers, regarding them as a security threat, and apply to divert footpaths out of sight of their homes.

The scale of the intrusion of new buildings all over the real countryside is such that much of southern England has taken on the character of a housing estate and even the mega-farms are industrial in appearance, looking like factory estates.

How should the modern-day Robert Hunter or Octavia Hill react? Theirs was always the radical approach. They would now embrace James Bryce and demand a right in law to roam across our native land. We have already been half-promised this. *"YOUR COUNTRY IS WORTH FIGHTING FOR,"* proclaimed scenic posters of the Second World War.

These were in his mind when Dr. Hugh Dalton, Attlee's Chancellor of the Exchequer, set up the National Land Fund to buy cherished pieces of landscape as a living memorial to the one-

and-half million men and women of the British Empire who had given their lives in two world wars. His was a linkage between the landscape and the romantic imagination, of the countryside being inspirational to poets and painters and therapeutic for the working and artisan classes.

It has been born again as the National Heritage Memorial Fund, though like the National Trust it underwent a phase of being the safety-net for country house art treasures – still not a preoccupation of ordinary people – rather than throwing influence and money at landscape preservation.

Ultimately, however, there has to be more to life and landscape beyond it and the National Trust. One day there will be a right to roam anywhere over our native land; God-given if you wish to be spiritual about it.

That is the moral right we have inherited which should be enshrined in law as a provision for access at will, on foot everywhere and by cycle or horse on suitable paths, across all open countryside. There is a compelling case for Parliament to give Britons an access passport.

Kate Ashbrook, secretary of the Open Spaces Society, suggested to the Access Review Working Party of the National Trust in 1993 that it should urge the Trust to put the Swedish "*Allemansratt*" into practice as "*a valuable experiment ... to see if there really are any problems*". The Trust, she urged with a deliberate pun, "*should be leading the way*" by showing all its land, "*even that with no access,*" on Ordnance Survey maps, and making special efforts to extend public use of its agricultural properties in lowland England:

"*On tenanted farmland, people should be given a right to wander over certain areas where they will do no harm. On all Trust properties there should be a presumption in favour of the widest possible public access, with restrictions only where it has been proved that the access is detrimental to landscape, archaeology or wildlife, and where this damage has been fully assessed.*"

Her hope is that the Trust will set the example in providing for the optimum level of countryside access. Deciding just which parts of the countryside should be accessible raises new problems. Open countryside is something we all know when we are in it, but anything approaching a quasi-legal description is fraught with difficulty.

If it comes to be defined then I would urge that *"open country"* is seen at its widest – to include mountains, moors, heaths, downs, riverbanks, meadows, woods, cliffs, and foreshore. Otherwise, denied our birthright, we may end up trying to achieve National Trust ownership over every single acre of half-decent landscape in the kingdom. It may make for attractive statistics but it is hardly a viable alternative.

The second crusade for a resurrected Octavia Hill would be to make the National Trust truly representative of the nation as a whole, rather than a clone of its membership, and trigger the enthusiasm of all categories and cultures that make up Britain's complex cosmopolitan mix. This the Trust is lamentably failing to do at present, with a expanding pensioner mebership occurring at the same time as a hemorrhaging of its much smaller under-23 category. Not only are young people failing to join the Trust in any numbers but neither are members of our considerable ethnic communities.

Farmer Chris Akrigg, the Trust's tenant on Buckden Pike in the Yorkshire Dales, reinforced my view that the National Trust membership is almost entirely white, aged and middle class. Just about every member arriving in the Dales comes into one of those categories, and many if not most are in all three. The same can be said of the Trust's 52-strong ruling council.

"You can see that from the cars," Mr Akrigg said. *"Spot the one that isn't a BMW! Not that it means they are very bright. I wonder how it is that they can drive cars with all those controls and yet fail to figure out how to open and close a gate."*

"That's because they can't find the button," John Pitfield explained.

On the other hand, Asian visitors do come with school

47

groups, and in particularly large numbers on farm open days. *"A lot of those kids had never seen farm animals before,"* Mr Akrigg continued, *"They had certainly never touched them."*

The absence, otherwise, of black and Asian faces is more than merely a reflection of the levels of disadvantage endemic in large sections of those communities. It is as if they have no cultural tradition of outdoor pursuits or countryside recreation. That is why the Trust must seek to stimulate their interest and knowledge.

Octavia Hill would point out that there was no custom of countryside access for all classes of the host community until her day, when the railways liberated the people to venture into the hills on the single afternoon a week that they were not working. Things have improved on that score but the National Trust is still only a fragile partnership between privilege and the people.

9—Cornish Stile.
Slabs of stone for steps.

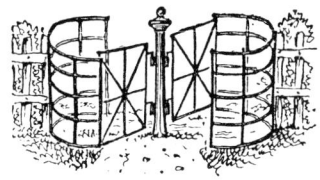

10—Double Iron Gates.
Each works independently.

11—Ladder Stile.
Rather dangerous.

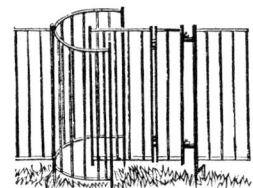

12—Footpath and Bridle Gate.
Can be opened out to admit cattle passing through. 4ft. high. To fold as above, £1 15s.; Gate only, not to fold, £1 10s.